The Rock and the Ripple

Written and Illustrated

By

Amy Caroline Andersen, M.S.E., NCC

I had a dream inside my head,

where all good things are done and said.

Text and illustrations copyright ©2013 by Amy Caroline Andersen

Published in 2013 by one girl one light, LLC. All rights reserved. No portion of this book may be reproduced, transmitted, or stored in an information retrieval system in any form or by any means, graphic, electronic, or mechanical, including photocopying, taping, and recording, without prior written permission from the publisher.

First edition 2013

Library of Congress Control Number: 2013912328

ISBN 978-0-9896807-0-7

Printed in Wisconsin

Book design by Kathy Gottlieb, Kaitlin Mueller, and Kevin Rau.

The illustrations were inspired by Miller's Bay, Lake Winnebago, Oshkosh, Wisconsin, and the beach in the city of Bray, County Dublin, Ireland.

Visit us at www.onegirlonelight.com

This book is dedicated to all the children of the world,

with a special dedication to my children,

Lauren, Shaun and Luke, and my granddaughter, Hayden.

Follow your dreams and spread love and hope through your ripples.

I walk by the lake every day.

This path I've walked in every way.

Today was different than other days.

Today was different in many ways.

Every day as I walk by,
I throw a stone and watch it fly.

Today I decided to try something new.
Today I believed…I hoped…I knew!

I had a dream inside my head,

where all good things are done and said.

I bent my body and scooped a rock.

I hopped three times upon one sock.

I closed my eyes and made a wish.

I gave a wink to all the fish.

I tossed that rock and heard the SWISH!

When I looked up it was no surprise,
the water had splashed clear up to the sky.
The fountain soaked a sleeping cloud,
who woke up startled and yelled real loud.

The noise it made had cleared the sky.
The sun shone through to make things dry.

People came out from all around,
filling the air with joyful sound.
All things lost were suddenly found.

All the scary things were gone.

All loud voices turned to song.

There was no longer a need for any fears,

the only things cried were happy tears.

No more hunger, hurt, or fighting.
No more thunder storms or lightning.
There was enough for all and even more.
No one had to lock their door.

Rainbows colored everyone's skin.
The whole world was each other's kin.

The dream I made with my one rock
rippled out from block to block.
Every person had a friend.
All things broken began to mend.
All good ripples never end.

So on a day when you believe it,

and in your heart can feel and see it.

Hold a dream inside your head,

where all good things are done and said.

Throw your rock and watch it ripple.

Watch the goodness start to triple.

Spread your dream from block to block.

Love will lead you to your rock!

For the parents:

"Few will have the greatness to bend history itself, but each of us can work to change a small portion of events, and in the total of all those acts will be written the history of this generation. Thousands of Peace Corps volunteers are making a difference in isolated villages and city slums in dozens of countries. Thousands of unknown men and women in Europe resisted the occupation of the Nazis and many died, but all added to the ultimate strength and freedom of their countries. It is from numberless diverse acts of courage and belief that human history is shaped. Each time a man stands up for an ideal, or acts to improve the lot of others, or strikes out against injustice, he sends forth a tiny ripple of hope, and crossing each other from a million different centers of energy and daring, those ripples build a current which can sweep down the mightiest walls of oppression and resistance."

— Senator Robert F. Kennedy, June 6th, 1966

Permission granted by the Robert F. Kennedy Center for Justice & Human Rights

Amy Caroline Andersen, M.S.E., NCC is the author-illustrator of *The Rock and the Ripple*. Amy is a college counselor, teacher, mother and grandmother. Amy is dedicated to helping make the world a more peaceful and joyful place by connecting people to each other through the power of reading and education, and to helping people of all ages feel their value and connect to their purpose.

Visit us at www.onegirlonelight.com